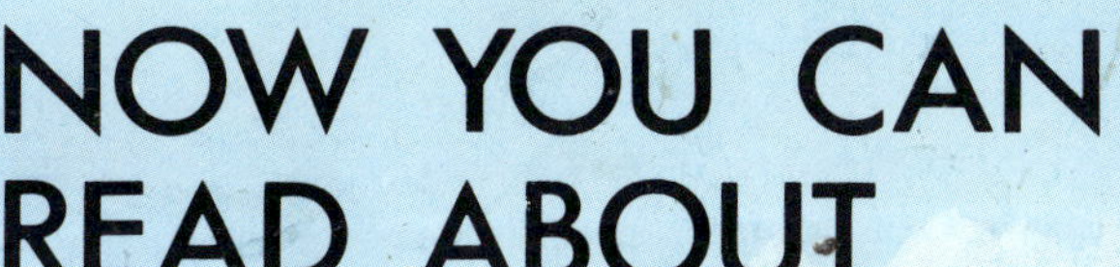
NOW YOU CAN
READ ABOUT...

CARS and TRUCKS

TEXT BY STEPHEN ATTMORE
ILLUSTRATED BY TONY GIBBONS

BRIMAX BOOKS • NEWMARKET • ENGLAND

These people are looking at the cars and trucks. These cars and trucks are for sale. Each year there are more cars on the roads. In some countries people drive on the left side of the road. In North America and Europe cars and trucks go on the right.

Trucks are used to carry loads. They move things from place to place. Some trucks are used to take goods from the factory to supermarkets and stores.

Look at the two cars. The small car cannot go very fast. It is better to drive a small car on short trips. It does not use as much fuel. The large car has more room inside. It can go fast. Some people like to drive big cars when they go on long journeys.

There are trucks to carry every sort of load. Trucks can go to almost any part of the world. The large truck is a juggernaut. It can carry large loads for long distances. The small truck carries little loads on short trips.

Here is one of the first cars ever made. It is over 80 years old. The brakes on this car are not very good. If you want to stop it on a hill, you use a sprag. It is like an anchor.

This car was made in America. It is a Model T Ford. Over 15 million of these cars were sold.

Here is a 1906 Rolls Royce Silver Ghost. The engine was so well made that it was as quiet as a ghost.

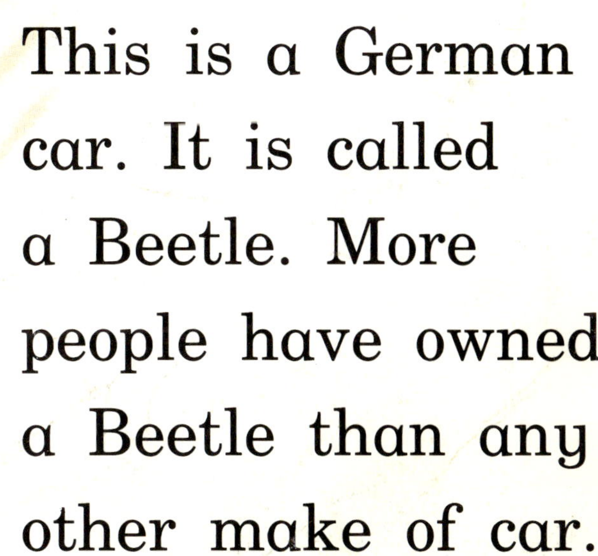

This is a German car. It is called a Beetle. More people have owned a Beetle than any other make of car.

Have you been to a car museum?

Here is one of the first trucks ever made. The driver and the goods are in the open. Look for the handle at the front of the truck. This is turned to start the engine. The wheels are wooden.

This American truck was made 70 years ago. It keeps the load and the driver dry. But it is cold for the driver in winter. Look for the gas lamp. This is the headlight. This truck has rubber tyres.

Look at this modern tanker. It is carrying a large load of fuel. Other tankers carry milk, wine or gases. The driver is talking to other drivers on a CB radio. The driver can sleep in the area at the back of the cab. Count the number of wheels on the truck.

This is inside a modern car. Look at all the dials. One dial shows the speed of the car. Another dial shows how much fuel there is left in the car. This car also has a computer. Its controls are to the right of the steering wheel. It can speak to you.

Most cars are built to travel on roads. But some cars can travel where there are no roads. You can drive this Range Rover car over rough ground. The engine has a lot of power. This car's tyres grip on land where other cars' tyres would get stuck.

Many trucks are used to carry loose loads like coal, sand and gravel. The yellow truck is called a dumper. Its strong engine pulls it over rough ground. The other truck is a tipper. It is not as strong. Tippers and dumpers can tip up their loads.

Lights flashing, sirens blaring – this is a road accident in Britain. The police are there first. They will try to find out what happened. Fire fighters are putting out the fire. Fire engines are special trucks. Ambulances, fire engines and police cars can go fast. They get to the scene of

an accident as soon as possible. The ambulance is taking the people who are hurt to hospital. These cars and trucks must have good engines. It is no help if they will not start or if they break down. People or animals may be in danger. Can you see the breakdown truck towing a car?

This is a sports car. There is only room inside for two seats. It can go fast. Rally cars drive along rough roads. The drivers try to get from one place to another as fast as possible.

The modern racing car is passing the old racing car. They are on a special track. You can see how racing cars have changed. Here is a strange car. It is called a drag racer. It goes very very fast.

What do you think cars and trucks will look like in the future? Here are some ideas. The long car is a special shape. This makes it go faster and saves fuel. The tyres are special too. They will not burst. The small car uses electricity for fuel.

This is what a truck of tomorrow might look like. Look at its shape. Its engine is quiet.

Now you have read about cars and trucks in this book. What are these cars and trucks used for?